PENITENTIARY RICH PRESENTS

AARON HERNANDEZ

THE UNTOLD PRISON STORY

REST IN PEACE CELL #57

by

KEIKO "SLIM" THOMAS

COPYRIGHT 2021 by: Penitentiary Rich, LLC.

All rights reserved. No part of this book may be used or reproduced in any manner without written permission from the copyright owner, except for the use of brief quotations for book reviews.

Cover art and Formatting:
Gram Telen
Book Cover and Layout Designer
⊕ www.fiverr.com/gramtelen

Published by:
Penitentiary Rich, LLC.
PO Box 860037
Plano, TX 75086
⊕ www.penitentiaryrich.com

Paperback ISBN: 978-7372262-3-9
Apple(ePUB) ISBN: 978-1-7372262-1-5
Kindle(mobi) ISBN:978-1-7372262-0-8

Printed in the United States of America

First Edition: June 2021

Dedication

To Aaron "Double A" Hernandez

"For God so loved the world he gave

his only begotten son"

John 3:16

Acknowledgments

I would like to take the time out and give special thanks to all those who contributed to this project, be it big or small. First, I would like to thank my fiancé, Alexis, for working on this manuscript night and day and quarterbacking my ideas and vision with the outside help. Also, thank you for investing your time, love, intelligence, and finances in me.Thanks for holding it down for me baby :) I LOVE YOU ALWAYS AND FOREVER. Thanks to my mother and father Beverly and Keith Thomas for being supportive and believing in me. A special thanks to my daughters Keianna and Tianna for giving me the motivation and willpower to succeed. Also, thanks to my stepdaughter London for making me laugh at her unique personality :). Special thanks to Ben for working with Lex on this project. I really appreciate it bro, thank you for being apart of this Penitentiary

Rich family. Thank you to Justin for your willingness to support this project and back many of the team ideas. Thanks bro! To my sister KayKay and Ashanti thank you for supporting me. To Tevin, thank you for picking up them collect calls and sending me money for commissary I love u bro. To Aubreus, thank you for being one of my financial advisors and book gurus :) its all love. Keema, I can't forget u I love u always. To the entire Thomas & Hackler family thanks for the support. I love y'all.(Rip Whitney Thomas) .To all my homies incarcerated here at Souza Baranowski aka "the max" bang your fucking doors. Free da guys!!!! Rest in peace cell 57.. To my Penitentiary Rich team thank you all.....

Table of Contents

1. Introduction 9
2. Memory: First Encounter 11
3. Memory: Accountability 15
4. Memory: Niggas on the Unit 17
5. Memory: Still Getting Money 21
6. Memory: Basketball 29
7. Memory: Night Life 31
8. Memory: The Whiteboy 35
9. Memory: Touchdowns & Tom Brady 41
10. Memory: Religion 43
11. Memory: Double Murder Trial 47
12. Memory: Double A Suicide 51
13. Memory: The Investigators 55
14. Memory: Shake Down 57
15. Memory: Bad Talking Double A 59
16. Memory: Letter To Double A 61
17. Memory: In My Opinion 65
About the Author 69

Introduction

In this book, I write down conversations and stories about a man who many in society saw as a cold-blooded killer. A man who in the prison world was seen as a fraud by many and a god by some. I had the privilege to get to know Double A in a short amount of time dating back to the beginning of 2017. We were housed on the same unit inside Souza-Baranowski, a population unit called G-2. I currently still reside at Souza-Baranowski Correctional Center.

In this book I will substitute real names for fictitious names. I will only use the real name Slim (which is myself), Double A (which is Aaron), and a few public figures he mentioned in our conversations. This is to protect the identities of my fellow convicts who may have been part of such a story or conversation. Some of these guys are still incarcerated and some are in the free world now.

INTRODUCTION

People have asked me all types of questions about Double A. They vary from, "What was his mentality like" to "Yo Slim, was he gay forreal?" There may be some shit you may want to know, but some shit I don't have answers to. In this book, I keep it 100% real and I'm sure you can find others to vouch for some of these stories, conversations, or the fact that I talked with Double A on the daily basis. As a matter of fact, he came to my cell door the night/morning before he committed suicide. Of course, the investigators wanted to know what was discussed between us.

I still remember that stupid ass question that they asked me, "Did he tell you that he was going to kill himself?" To this day, I still think to myself WTF.

Reader please beware that I write according to how I speak. I do not use big fancy words and I'm not trying to become a best-seller. I just happen to be the author of my memories.

Rest in peace to my nigga, Double A.

That being said, come and take this walk with me down memory lane.

First Encounter

One day I'm in the prison yard, shooting the shit with a couple homies. We just out in the yard catching rec and shit. I've probably been on the unit for maybe two or three days. A couple of the homies was giving me the rundown on the block and shit. You know, telling me who's who and what's what. I remember scoping the yard out and seeing the nigga, Double A, working out by himself. I was with one of my niggas at the time, I'll give him the name Hood-Hop. Laugh out loud, cause he definitely hood-hop but that's another story. Anyway, me and Hood-Hop walk the track, you know just doing a couple laps. We talking about bitches, money, and you know thinking back on the lifestyle we once lived. Guess who walks up on a nigga? Yeah, you guessed it. The nigga Double A. Him and the nigga Hood-Hop was cool already.

FIRST ENCOUNTER

Double A asked "Yo, what's good with you niggas? Can I spend?"

Man, I look at this nigga like what, walk with us? Remind you this is Mr. Celebrity - the multimillion-dollar nigga. My man, Hood-Hop, told him, "Yeah bro. We just walking laps and kicking it. This is my nigga, Slim. Slim, this is my nigga, Double A". This nigga Double A looks at me, smiles, and sticks his hand out for a handshake.

I shakes the nigga hand. "What's good bruh?"

The first thing the nigga say to me out his mouth was, "Yo, do you bang?"

I was smiling but thinking in my head, is this nigga serious? I replied, "Yeah, I'm a Gangster Disciple," throwing my pitchforks in the air for emphasis.

He responded, "Oh okay, I'm Blood."

"I heard."

"I'm Double A."

"I'm Slim," I replied.

"Yo, ain't Lil Blood your celly?" He asked while he looked at me.

I responded, "yeah".

He says, "yeah, I been watching how you move. I like that. You don't be fucking with mad niggas."

"Nah, I don't," I replied with my eyes searching the yard for my celly, now that this nigga mentioned him. Remind you most of the niggas in the yard lowkey watching this nigga every move. Some out of aspiration but most with the look of envy.

"Yo, Lil Blood told me me that you got mad books. What you into, what you be building on?" asked Double A.

I think I replied something like, "Shit my nigga I try and read everything. That way I know a little about a lot."

That nigga started laughing saying, "Yeah, Hood-Hop. I fuck with Slim". By the time yard was over, it's fair to say we became cool after picking each other's brain.

Accountability

I remember another time me and this nigga Double A was walking the yard, just politicking about prison and shit. Out of nowhere, Double A says "Bro let me ask you some?"

I'm like, "what's good?"

He looks at me and said, "Yo, do you believe everything happens for a reason?"

I think before replying and I say, "yeah, I do. Why you ask though?"

I remember him shaking his head from side to side. I can tell that he was doing some deep thinking because he went silent. "How much time you doing, Slim?" he asked me, breaking the silence.

"I'm doing 17 to 19 years with 3 years of probation." I replied.

"You got to stay focused and don't give up. Keep the same energy you got now my nigga. You gone win", he said, looking at me and sounding all sincere and shit.

I replied, "Hope so, my nigga."

"You know I learned in life, we have to take accountability for our own actions. We can't play the blame game you feel me? I take accountability for Double A actions. I ain't mad at nobody for my current situation. I'm the sole controller of my life, you heard me?" he said.

I'm like, "Yeah but sometimes other peoples actions can have an effect on your life."

That nigga looked at me with a look that said come on, bro. "At the end of the day, it's all on you. I went from the penthouse suites to cell #57."

Niggas on the Unit

To be honest, I've always been a cool nigga. You know, nothing more or nothing less. But when I started associating with Double A on the daily basis though, my status started to rise on a new level. I never was boasting or bragging that I was cool with the nigga. Let me remind you, I'm a gangster. I stand on my own rep. My name is my name and niggas know how I'm coming. I never been a dick rider. I think that's another reason Double A took a liking to me. I was always nonchalant, you feel me? I never tried to make him like me or try and force myself in his presence.

Believe me, a lot of niggas was on straight groupie time ror real. Man, I had COs trying to be cool with me because they knew that me and Double A was cool. That shit was wild.

I remember niggas on the unit use to walk up to me like, "what's good," trying to start conversation in hopes that if they get cool with me, they will be cool with Double A. That shit never worked though.

Niggas used to be like "Yo Slim, what's up with that nigga?"

I used to say, "Shit, that nigga cool."

If you saw this nigga on the unit, you'd probably think "yo, this dude is forcing it." The nigga was all the way street through from his conversations to his swag. I remember this Crip nigga that was on our unit. This nigga, Double A, hated this nigga, forreal. He didn't hate dude because he was a Crip. He hated the Crip because he was always loud as fuck. The Crip was one of them niggas that acted like he was bout that until it was go time. It's fair to say that the Crip was a straight "red nose" clown.

Double A used to always be like, "Yo bro look at this clown ass nigga."

Most niggas on the unit would sneak diss on the nigga Double A all the time. Of course, he was never aware of the sneak dissing. He would've definitely addressed the shit. The nigga Double A wasn't a "bitch" and he always had a point to prove if a nigga tried him. If anybody tell you different, they lying.

Still Getting Money

I remember this nigga Double A asking a dude one day, did his people send that money to his people. Remind you, I overheard this shit. I been knowing this nigga for like a month and a half. In my head, I'm trying figure out how in the fuck do this nigga owe Double A some money.

"Yeah, my people sent a money order yesterday," replied ol' boy Double A was talking to.

"Alright, I'm about to get on the phone in a minute. I'll holla at you soon as I get off," Double A said as he was walking towards my cell door.

"What's good, my nigga?" I asked him once he stopped at my cell door.

"Aint' Shit bro. What y'all niggas doing in there?" He replied, looking in my cell. He was trying to see what was up with me and my celly.

"Shit bro, I'm doing laundry real quick. This nigga Lil Blood watching tv." I said looking towards the nigga Lil Blood.

"Yo, you smoke?" asked Double A.

"My nigga, what kind of question is that?" I shot back at the nigga.

He starts laughing and tell me to give him a minute and he'll be right back.

"Bet," I said tapping the door. *Prison gesture*

The nigga Double A pulls back on me five minutes later and hands me a folded piece of paper and says, "do whatever you want with it." Then he leaves and goes to get on the phone.

I open the paper and saw 50 squares on a strip of paper. Remind you, this is worth a couple hundred dollars in prison and the homie just gave me that shit. I cut 5 squares off and gave that to Lil Blood. Then I cut five more squares off and rolled up five j's. To be honest, they call this shit K2, but niggas don't have a real clue what the fuck this shit is. I call the shit "chemicals" because it's a mixture of chemicals on paper and when you smoke that shit, you get dumb high. I'm talking Jupiter.

Later on that day, I ended up finding out that the nigga Double A was "trapping." I never went straight up to Double A and asked him was he trapping though. I knew that eventually he would tell me.

Sure enough, a couple days go by and he's asks, "Yo Slim, what you got a store?" The only reason he asked me this was because of the niggas pulling up to my cell back to back leaving with canteen items.

"Yeah I got a store, my nigga. You know I'm just trying to live. A nigga get tired of asking on the street for bread. You feel me?" I replied, letting that nigga see the seriousness expressed on my face.

"Yeah, I see you got this bitch bumping like the traphouse," he laughed.

"Yo, you balling up tonight at the gym?" I asked him switching up the subject.

"Nigga, hell yeah, you know these niggas gone be talking mad shit if we duck action on that court" he replied looking and pointing towards the poker table.

"Yeah, especially that nigga with the dreads," I said while pointing out one of the best ballers on the Boston team.

Later that day we was getting ready to go to the gym and Double A slips me a folded piece of paper.

I asked, "What's this bro?"

He replied, "Stash that. That's you." I put that shit in one of my hiding spots. We're on our way to the gym and the only thing on my mind at this time is trying to find out what's in that pack. After spending 2.5 hours in the gym, we returned to our unit. I head straight to the shower and jumped on the phone afterward. We only have 30 minutes in total and this is our last rec for the night. Once I'm in my cell for the night, I go to the stash. This pack was a little bigger than the pack he gave me with the K2. I opened up the pack and a nigga was all smiles.

This nigga, Double A, just hit me off with a 10pk suboxin strips. In my head, I'm thinking, "yeah ain't no looking back now."

"Yo, Lil Blood... Here," I said handing my cellmate a strip.

"G.L.O., my nigga" he replied smiling. That nigga Lil Blood wasted no time breaking his shit up. "Yo, where the spoons at, my nigga?" Lil Blood was looking on the desk for a spoon.

"It's one in the cup by the tv, Blood" I replied, putting my pack back in my stash.

"Yo, you fucking around?" I remember Lil Blood asking me, putting some get high on the spoon.

"Nah I'm good bro" I replied.

I remember the next morning I handed Double A a kite. I was just letting him know that I appreciated him for looking out and shit. He was cool with Youngblood and they both was "Blood." I knew he didn't want Youngblood knowing his moves. I also know that he didn't fuck with the nigga Blood on that level. Blood was a gangster, but he never threw salt or hate. I mean, at least not around me. Blood was short timing anyway. He was going home in a couple months. I know some of you niggas might be like, "Yo, thats fucked up he was fucking with you on that level but not his homie." First off, I don't owe none of y'all no explanation. Let's get that straight off the rip. Second, that nigga Blood just wasn't a hustler. PERIOD!

Anyway, days go by, we getting money, everything is everything. Every prisoner in the building know that G2 was litty. Niggas receiving kite after kite, you heard. All type of niggas trying to get they hands on that "get high". Plus them numbers was super low at the time. I remember one day niggas was high off a stick of that "code 99". That's a code in the prison system for man down, so you know niggas was high as shit.

"Yo superstar" I said, calling the nigga Double A by the nickname that I gave him.

"Nigga, what I tell you about calling me that shit?" He said aggravated but still laughing.

"Nigga, why the fuck you in here hustling?", I asked that nigga, straight out ignoring his question.

"My nigga, what type of question is that?" He asked me, this time looking at me serious as if my question offended him.

"Bro, why are you trapping? I know you ain't pressed for no bread. These niggas round here keep telling. Therefore, the IPS keep running in niggas spot," I shot back at that nigga, aggravated that he became aggravated.

"What, you a pocket watcher now nigga? How you know what I'm pressed for? Let me guess, you into all that Fox25 news shit too, huh? I didn't think you was one of them niggas, Slim."

I can't even describe that nigga's look when he said that shit to me. I remember him just shaking his head from side to side. "Yeah, you right bro. You got that. That ain't my business you feel me," I replied.

"Yo bro, this shit is play money. Just cause a nigga got paper doesn't mean he trying to spend his shit, you feel me?" He said, feeling like he needed to explain himself for why he was doing the shit he was doing.

"I hear you bro. That shit is just foreign to me. I don't know too many niggas that's high profile, celebrity status, niggas who have touched millions, you feel me," I replied, keeping it real with my nigga.

"Nah, my nigga. I understand. You see it as 'I'm rich' type shit and if you was me, you wouldn't be doing what I'm doing," he said, letting me know he now understood my line of questioning.

"Exactly," I replied. I can't lie, sometimes I used to look at this nigga and wonder to myself was he semi-retarded?

I know the nigga was bipolar but shit, they say the same about me. Honestly, at times, I was curious to know what was going on in his head. I have seen this nigga Doubla A check other convicts for $50, asking them niggas like, "where my money at?"

I told you in the beginning I'm going to keep it 100% in this book. So yeah, something about this nigga Double A was off. He was a little weird, for real. I was always trying to figure him out but sometimes dude was like a fish out of water. Not for nothing, we definitely got that schmoney though.

Basketball

Yo, on the gym days, we use to always play five on five full court. Double A and I was always on the same team. We had major basketball smoke with Boston. I'm not going to front on them niggas from the bean though, most of them niggas was nice. Double A and I was a force though. I'm 6'5 and weigh about 190, "Slim." Double A was 6'4 and weighing around 220 "cut up".

On the court, there's nothing that I can't do. I can handle, pass, shoot, and my defense is super crazy. I know I'm nice as shit, no cap. This nigga, Double A though, man, this nigga probably could have made it pro in basketball too. This nigga was wicked nice and he could jump.

I remember throwing this nigga alley-oops from half court. There were times we lost damn near every game though, but most times we won every game. That nigga

Double A would tell me, "Slim bro, you should be in the fucking NBA somewhere".

I just laughed it off like, "I know, right." One day after playing a couple of games, I told Double A, "Nigga I wish I could get them videos of our games and sell them to TMZ".

That nigga was like, "yeah, Harvey will love those". We both were laughing it up. However, I was dead ass serious, if I could get my hands on those tapes then I would've sold them shits top dollar.

Night Life

I use to always ask that nigga to tell me stories about that night life. Every time I asked him to tell a story, Double A would always laugh and be like, "What kind of story you want?"

"My nigga gve me a penthouse, top floor looking down at the city lights, high off fame, bad bitches around me, 'I'm that nigga' story." I always knew that he really liked telling those stories. He knew that most of us wanted a chance to experience that shit so that always gave him a one up on us. Not that he was the type of nigga to try and shit on niggas. He just knew that once he got in story mode, he would command the room.

I remember this one story that became one of my favorites. I used to always make him tell this shit because this shit was like an audiobook. This nigga, Double A, told me that one time him and a couple of his niggas was out in Las Vegas partying.

He said he had like $30,000 cash in his pocket plus he had all type of "swipe money." That's what he called his credit cards. He said they had all types of drugs coke, percs, molly, and weed. You know them niggas superstars and shit so they all jewelz up, nigga's wrists and necks crowded with diamonds.

The nigga said they were top floor penthouse and the whole room was glass everywhere. The walls was glass and a big ass pool on the balcony. There were all types of bitches, running in and out that bitch. Every bitch that got in the pool had to get in naked. I remember him being like, "we in Vegas and you know in Vegas people don't sleep."

When this nigga told his stories, he painted them shits for real. He said him and his people having a good time and he notice one of his niggas isn't in the room. He like, "yo, I'm looking for this niggas and shit."

He said he went to the bathroom, opened the door, and his man got six bitches in there on some straight 'porno.com' shit. Everybody was naked. It's a walk in shower, mad bitches is in there kissing, sucking, etc."

His man asked, "You in?"

He said "Nah nigga, I'm good. I was just looking for you," and went back in the room where everybody was at.

I always asked the nigga why he ain't fuck them hoes that was in the bathroom with his man, but he told me, "Bro, when you become a boss, that shit ain't bout none. Pussy starts falling out the sky along with money."

That shit always made me laugh.

Double A said when he went back into the party and sniffed a couple lines of yayo, he was all geeked up and now feeling on top of the world.

He yelled out, "WHO WANTS THIS DICK" and bitches started turning into vultures and shit. He said them hoes started fighting each other for the dick. He had hoes sniffing cocaine off his dick, you heard.

One bitch started crying and shit. Double A asked, "What's wrong?"

She said, "Nothing. I'm just happy God answered my prayers tonight."

He was like, "What?"

And the bitch said "I got to suck yo dick!"

Obviously, I don't remember the whole story, word for word. So I know I'm missing other details but that was my favorite part. I know some of you niggas like, "Man niggas do that shit in the hood on the daily!" Let's be real, nigga. Ain't no bitch never ever start crying because she got to suck your dick. OL HATING ASS NIGGA.

The Whiteboy

Now I ain't going to lie that Whiteboy and Double A was super tight. The Whiteboy admitted that he was gay, by the way. I know the nigga Double A would have killed for that dude, straight up. I highly doubt them niggas was engaging in any homosexual activities. I never saw them niggas alone in no closed room together or no shit like that. Just so I'm clear, the Whiteboy admitted to being gay after Double A committed suicide. When Double A was around, he never showed any signs of homo or bisexual shit.

The Whiteboy was running around claiming "Blood" too but rumor has it, them Bloods had kicked him out the set. I never seen the nigga Double A all geeked up off the drugs like the Whiteboy. Keeping it 100%, that nigga

Double A had that monkey on his back. Although, I know some niggas that's way worse.

I remember one time the Whiteboy got so damn high that he was stuck in front of Double A cell. This nigga Double A was on the top tier, on the high side in #57. The Whiteboy and him were leaning against the top tier railing. They both had just hit their 'homemade' pipe. The crazy part about that was the CO was screaming lock in because rec was over. The Whiteboy was stuck against the rail and couldn't move.

When everybody started locking in the CO noticed the Whiteboy all out of place, stuck on stupid. The CO walks up the stairs and starts calling the Whiteboy by his name. The Whiteboy was just holding onto the railing, stuck.

"We have a code 99 in G2." announced the prison intercom.

"Man down, man down, nigga smoking that gas" screamed a couple convicts. Moments later, more COs came with a nurse pushing the medical stretcher. "UBER! UBER! THAT NIGGA NEED A UBER!" yelled more convicts.

Man, you had to see this nigga, for real. This nigga started twitching and foaming out the mouth. Double A started calling the Whiteboy name but the Whiteboy couldn't hear him because he was flying with the birds. They put the Whiteboy on the stretcher and wheeled him into HSU (that's the medical unit). The COs was hip to what was wrong with him because that shit happens on the daily basis around here.

I also remember a couple weeks after Double A committed suicide the Whiteboy was under full court pressure. Every channel on the TV was saying he and the nigga was lovers and all type of shit.

So you know niggas was like, "Whiteboy, they talking about you on the news," and "Yo! Yall niggas was fucking and sucking?"

Remind you, the Whiteboy is inside the cell on the mother fucking unit, and he ain't saying shit. Everybody is cracking jokes and shit like, "Yo man, tell me it ain't so!"

That nigga said, "Yeah, that was my man..." Niggas was like awh hell noooo, you feel me.

I thought the Whiteboy was just capping and doing anything to claim some fame. They had the Whiteboy all on the news everyday talking about his love affair with Double A.

I remember watching Dr. Pill when Double A fiancé was on there and shit. Dr. Phil asked her if she knew if Double A was gay of not. She answered "No." Then Dr. Phil asked her did she know about the Whiteboy and did Double A ever mention him? She replied by repeating the Whiteboy name in disgust and said, "I never heard of him!"

Yo, the unit erupted in laughter and everybody is going crazy. Remind you, we watching this shit and the Whiteboy is watching this shit too. The Whiteboy was sick to his stomach that he was exposed in prison and on national TV. This nigga reputation is done. Finished. Stick a fork in it.

See, for those who don't know this nigga, he really thought he was gang gang. The nigga was popping 5s and shit. That dude was exposed and Double A probably did flips in his grave once Whiteboy made the announcement.

I remember Dr. Phill asking Double A fiancé was there any letter written to the Whiteboy? She replied, "No Double A didn't write him".

For those of you who don't know it was rumors, that Double A wrote 3 letters, one for his fiancé, one for his daughter, one for the Whiteboy. It was "facts" that he wrote three letters, but the Whiteboy was never written.

Double A said he was going to give him a watch. At least the Whiteboy was claiming that. It was said to be facts that Double A wrote three letters, one for his mom, fiancé and, daughter. The nigga Double A wasn't dead for a week and this nigga was trying to capitalize on a watch.

I remember the Whiteboy getting knocked out like a week after Double suicide. Why he get knocked out? That nigga owed this Vice Lord a couple of dollars for some get high. The Whiteboy had some balls because the Vice Lord ran down on him like, "Where my money?"

The Whiteboy said, "Ain't got shit for you?"

Crack, bam, blap, down go Frazier, down go Frazier. The Vice Lord beat the shit out of that Whiteboy. Somebody ended up snitching though because the Whiteboy owed some other niggas too and the Vice Lord took dude whole canteen bag. On top of that, the Whiteboy face was all fucked up.

I think that shit made it kinda hot too. The IPS snatched up the Whiteboy and played detective. I'm guessing they ran the cameras back cause I don't want to speculate and throw dirt on someones name, so he get the benefit of the doubt. They came back and snatched up the Vice Lord though. He and the Whiteboy did box time. The Vice Lord ended up coming back to the unit but I never saw the Whiteboy again.

Touchdowns & Tom Brady

I asked Double A about Tom Brady all the time. That nigga always smile saying, "Greatness." He use to tell me how privileged he was to catch passes from Brady. He always spoke good on his name. "Yo Slim. That nigga, Brady, the truth. For real. And he a cool dude, believe it or not." He would always say to me.

I would ask, "What was he like off the field?"

Double A always would laugh at me like I was stupid. He would say, "Man them niggas didn't fuck with me like that." He would say to me how he was an outcast amongst the Patriots. I think he liked being the outcast though. He used to be like, "Man them niggas thought I was crazy, bro."

I believed that nigga too because how he was thugging in here. I just couldn't see him hanging with niggas like Tom Brady or Gronk. This nigga was definitely on another level compared to them dudes. He never really spoke on the Patriots though or football in general. I mean if someone would ask him about his former team, he would comment on them. I always heard him speak good. I don't know if it was because he was surrounded by diehard fans or what. Now that I think about it, I don't even think I seen him watch a football game, for real.

"How it feel to score a touchdown in the NFL nigga?" I remember asking him one time.

"You ever try cocaine?" He asked me.

"I tried it," I said downplaying the fact that I used the drug several times.

"Well that feeling times five." I remember him saying, using his arms to express to me what he was saying. One thing about that nigga though, he was always smiling.

Religion

This was a topic we always talked about because we both studied multiple religions. I think Double A was Catholic or Christian though. Whichever one he was, he definitely had doubts about it.

I remember him being thirsty to learn about the Five Percenter teachings. I was just getting knee deep in the lessons. So I use to build with him about some of the knowledge I was studying. He use to eat that shit up. He was loving that knowledge of self. He would say, "Peace God." That nigga used to really feel that knowledge.

I used to want to hear a celebrity story and that nigga wanted to hear about the nation of Gods and Earth. We used to kick it about the Bible a lot too. I remember how shocked he was to learn how I was well read when it came to the scriptures. I remember him asking me a question one day pertaining to why I was a Five Percenter. I told him that I'm not a Five Percenter and that my religion is "Islam." So he asked me was I Muslim. "Yeah, I took my Shahada." Then I told him, I Study Life Around Me = ISLAM and he told me that was deep.

It was another dude on the unit who also studied multiple religions. Double A use to build with him a lot too. I remember one day I'm talking to Double A and I notice that his TV isn't in his cell. I asked him, "Where yo TV at?" That's when he told me that dude was using it. Right then and there I knew that he fucked with dude hard.

I remember when he committed suicide, they found bible scriptures on the wall and COs said he had John 3:16 written on his forehead. His cell was closed off for two weeks or longer after he died. Once they opened his cell up to clean it up and allow the next inmate to move in, I saw the writing on the wall. I'll never forget how he would always talk about sacrifices. He used to compare himself to Jesus Christ, but not on a religious level. He would say we all have Jesus Christ inside of us.

He would say, "When it's time to make sacrifices, would you give your life to save the people you love? Would you forgive those who have crossed you? Everything happens for a reason. Maybe this is how my life is meant to end?"

Honestly, I always thought maybe he was just thinking on a grandiose scale. Maybe he was just self-reflecting and soul searching. After his death, I realized that he was preparing himself for a sacrifice. He was telling me in so many words, but it was up to me to connect the dots.

Double Murder Trial

Over the years of me being incarcerated I have met and talked with all types of killers. I have looked in the eyes of some and saw no life, no light, not even a soul. Normally, when someone's facing life in prison, it's kind of hard to smile. Simply because your game-face is on, and your life is in the hands of a group of people whose lifestyle is nothing like yours.

I have seen Double A keep a smile on his face every single day, including when he was on trial for his double murder. This dude never showed any signs of doubt. You never would catch this nigga looking worried or stressed out. He was always confident and say, "Bro, shit was meant to be like this for me. This my story, my life, this is my legacy."

I just used to say to myself, "Yo, this nigga is crazy." That nigga was in the middle of his double murder trial, acting cool as a fan. Remind you, they have this nigga "life" on his first murder conviction. That nigga be playing basketball like he ain't even on trial.

"Nigga, my lawyer about to smack this shit bro," he would say anytime a nigga wish him well on the verdict. I remember the day they came back with the verdict, we was like eight deep in a cell smoking and shit, niggas tuned in paying close attention. Everybody in the room fuck with Double A, we nervous as shit, you feel me. At least eight of us in the room was convicted of murder or had gone through a similar situation.

The room was quiet as shit once the foreman of the jury started speaking, "The jury finds Aaron Hernandez of murder in the first degree of first victim, NOT guilty." We all erupted with excitement.

"Hold up, hold up, be quiet," I said to the room.

"We the jury find Aaron Hernandez, of murder in the first degree of second victim, NOT guilty."

I remember everybody started hugging each other and laughing, the homie had just beat that shit. This nigga Double A was on the TV smiling in the courtroom, hugging and shaking hands with his attorney. I saw his family crying tears of joy. The whole unit was going crazy, shit was wild.

That nigga Double A came back to the unit at like seven thirty or some that night. As soon as he came on the unit, niggas went crazy kicking the doors and screaming. I remember that nigga smiling ear to ear just soaking it all up.

"Yeah I told y'all niggas man, didn't I tell y'all? Two down, one to flip nigga!" He was screaming out.

I remember us going to the gym the next day, you know everybody is still excited. It's always good to see a nigga win in any situation when it's us vs the state or the feds. Double A was smiling, but didn't seem super happy like the day before.

Before we started playing basketball, I told him, "Yeah congrats again, my nigga." And gave him dap with a hug.

After we embraced he said, " I told you to never give up. Everything happens for a reason. It ain't over with yet. I'm still here."

After our 2.5 hours was up, we was on our way back to our unit. Once we got back to our unit, this nigga, Double A starts handing out all type of food and books. He let the religious dude I told you about earlier hold down his tv. This shit he normally will do because he was weird like that nobody questioned what was up with him.

I remember him coming to me and Lil Blood's cell like "Yo what's good with you niggas?"

I told him, "Shit... What's good with you?"

That nigga said, "Yo, let me get y'all contact info in case something happens and we split up, we can always be in contact." So we gave him our contact info and he did the same.

"Have a good night bro," me and Lil Blood told him.

"Y'all too. I'm coming through in the AM," he replied heading to his cell to lock in. Those was the last words he spoke to me.

TOP SECRET

Double A Suicide

"Slim, Slim, yo, Slim wake up bro!" Screamed Lil Blood tapping on my bunk.

"Yo nigga, what the fucks up!" I asked, pissed off that he just woke me up.

"Yo that nigga Double A 'code99' smoking that shit."

"What?" I asked dumbfounded.

"Nigga look!" Lil Blood said pointing towards Double A's cell. I got up and went to the door. I saw like four COs and two nurses that had Double A on the stretcher, pumping his chest.

"Code 99 man down, niggas smoking that gaspack!" Yelled convicts over the tier.

I remember one of my niggas saying, "Yo Double A! It's me, Rozay! Wake up, my nigga, wake up." Niggas had no idea how serious this shit was at the time. Everybody thought that he probably passed out from smoking that shit. Nobody at the time knew that he committed suicide.

"Yo, Lil Blood! He naked on the stretcher." I remember saying to my celly, confused as to why he's naked on the stretcher.

"Yeah I know," Lil Blood said. "Yo, they giving him mouth to mouth!"

Somebody yelled out, "Yo I think he tried to kill himself!"

"I see a piece of sheet hanging from the window!" Somebody else yelled.

I was looking at the nurse doing CPR on Double A and his arm just went limp off the stretcher. My gut told me he was dead. I remember my grandmother telling me something years ago. She said, "some people like to go out the same way they came in... NAKED."

"Yo, Lil Blood, the homie's dead my nigga." I remember saying to Lil Blood, sounding super sad and depressed.

"Why you say that?" Lil Blood was asking me. By this time they was carrying him down on the stretcher.

"Look at him," I remember telling Lil Blood. I moved away from the door so he could see for himself.

"Damn man. I hope not," he replied with tears coming from his eyes. I can't lie my eyes was filling up with water too. One look at Lil Blood and the tears started to roll down my cheek.

The unit was super quiet now, everybody realized how serious the situation had become. The million dollar question was ,"Why did this nigga attempt a suicide?" I say attempt because it still wasn't confirmed just yet what really happened. One thing for sure, we was soon to find out.

After they rushed him to the medical unit, the whole block was up having conversation, trying to figure out why? Remind you it three something in the morning so you could see the flashing lights from the ambulance and police cars.

"Channel 25 Fox News" somebody yelled on the tier. "Breaking news!"

Double A had just been pronounced dead.

I'm in total shock at this point. Why? Nobody really knows but we have our theories though. I remember trying to decipher every conversation that me and Double A had. I was trying to connect the dots. Nothing stood out to me at that moment. The prison was locked in following Double A's suicide. The investigators hit our block hard. They start questioning us one by one.

TOP SECRET

The Investigators

Investigator: Good morning, your name is Keiko Thomas correct?

Slim: Yes

Investigator: We have camera footage of Aaron Hernandez receiving something from your cell minutes before he locked in. What was it?

Slim: My contact information.

Investigator: We have been told by IPS that you are a close associate of Aaron Hernandez. Is that true?

Slim: We was cool.

Investigator: Do you know if he was religious?

Slim: I don't know.

Investigator: Did he do drugs?

Slim: Not that I know of.

Investigator: We are sorry about your friend. Can you tell us any information that could help our investigation?

Slim: No sir, I am shocked and lost as well.

Investigator: Alright Mr. Thomas. If anything sticks out to you please contact the IPS.

Slim: Alright.

Investigator: Thank you

Right as I was about to leave out the room the other detective spoke up.

Investigator #2: Did you know he was planning to kill himself?

Slim: What the fuck, hell NO!

I looked at this nigga like looks could kill and I shook my head in disgust walking out the door.

Shake Down

They did a major shakedown following Double A suicide. COs from all over Massachusetts DOC was all over the unit. They had the K9 unit, state troopers, detectives, and all types of law enforcement. You know, Double A was "high profile." Plus his family and lawyers wanted to know what happened. Somebody job was on the line.

"Shake down, shake down, K9, X-ray machines. Yo, they deep" yelled out a couple of convicts from behind their cell doors. I remember hearing mad toilets flush, niggas was stashing and throwing away all contraband.

They made everybody strip and the whole routine. They made us put on scrubs and shower slippers. Next, they started escorting all of us to the gym. We stayed in the gym for maybe 2 to 3 hours.

We returned to the unit and looking like, "what the fuck?" These bitch ass motherfuckers destroyed everybody cell. Some niggas ain't make it back to the unit though. As soon as they're walking down that long ass hallway coming from the gym, them people had a piece of paper and they was picking niggas off. I remember two of my niggas ain't make it back. Supposedly the cops said they found a knife and K2. Shit was real wild.

I think we was locked in for like a week and a half, maybe two weeks. I forget the exact number of days. I know a lot of niggas wasn't feeling that lockdown shit. Especially after the first 72 hours, niggas was turning up because they wanted to talk to their loved ones.

TOP SECRET

Bad Talking Double A

My nigga Double A wasn't dead for a week when niggas started to come out their mouths sideways. Niggas started calling Double A all types of bitch ass niggas. They were saying, "Man let us out. Fuck that nigga. Niggas die everyday." I remember niggas saying, "If that was a regular nigga, we would've been out already."

Double A was the topic in the prison I know for at least three months straight. I was cool with Double A, that was my nigga but during that time I was still in a state of shock. I remember calling a couple of niggas out for speaking bad about the dead.

Everybody had some to say, now that Double A was dead. Niggas that wouldn't have even looked in his direction, all of a sudden got heart overnight.

That shit still don't sit right with me though. I get uncomfortable just thinking about the shit. I know for a fact that nigga Double A would've punished you niggas that was bad talking his name. I still got tension with a couple niggas over that shit.

Letter To Double A

Double A,

What's good my nigga? I wish that we could have met under different circumstances, but unfortunately that wasn't our case. Our lifestyles was much different, but our mentality was much the same. At the end of the day we ended up in the same place. I remember when I first saw you on the news. I said to myself, "Look at this dumbass nigga."

"Why the fuck would he go and do some shit like that?" Everybody in America probably wanted to know the answer to that question. Unknown to me at the time, I think I got the million dollar answer from the million dollar man himself. I think back on conversations we had. I have come to realize that you really can't judge a book by its cover. I remember how you used to tell me how I'm more that just a street nigga, and in order to get to that next level, I gotta stay focused on whatever I'm doing. Really want it.

I remember you telling me, "Slim, unless you try and do something beyond the shit you have already mastered, you will never grow." Before I met you, I wanted to live the life you lived. I wanted the money and the fame too. Sometimes I asked myself had I become successful like you, would I have ended up in a position like you did? I think the answer would be more likely a yes than a no.

But still, throughout our short time together, you taught me a lot. I remember you telling me how much shit you learned from me, but I never got to tell you how much I learned from you. If I knew that last conversation was our last one, I would have told you how much I valued our friendship. I would have told you to not give up and to keep fighting. I would have told you to remain humble in the face of adversity. I would have said think of a different route. Had I known what was going on inside your head, I would have tried to help you. I would've extended my hand, if I saw you stumbling.

I now know that your smile was just to throw off and hide how you was really feeling. Me, along with everybody else that was around you, just assumed you was good. We figured that you was Aaron Hernandez, the celebrity, you got no worries. Man every time I saw you, I saw you smiling. I never saw you down. I never witnessed you have a bad day. I know how that it had to be super hard on you, especially having to be the center of attention all the time. I understand why you put that pain deep inside because, on the outside, you can't let you fellow convicts or the media see you down.

If I could talk to you one last time, I'd tell you that I now understand it all. Some people may never know the answers why you did what you did.

"Sacrifices." For God so loved the world, he gave his only begotten son. I know that you would have gave your blessings to publish these memories inside this book. I just wanted the world to get to know a little about the Double A that I knew. Rest in peace, my friend.

The homie,
$lim

In My Opinion

My name is Keiko Thomas, aka "Slim," for those who don't know. I'm sure you probably have never heard of me, but you heard of my man Double A, right? The former New England Patriot. Yeah, that's him, the dude who committed suicide in the maximum penitentiary. The dude who was convicted of murder and found not guilty on two different murder charges.

What? Why you talking about my homie in a negative light? You didn't even know him? What he do to you? Oh, I'm a piece of shit? Why you say that? Yeah, I was facing murder charges too. Yea, I was facing robbery charges and gun charges too. How you know that? Yeah, I was facing home invasion too.

Damn! What you police? You a detective? I should have known some of you badge wearing motherfuckers was going to buy my book. You wanted to see what I was going to talk about, huh? Well I didn't break the law, did I?

Laugh out loud. Yeah, I'm an auther now, I'm not a murderer. Well, I mean, hold up... Technically, I'm doing 17 to 19 years for manslaughter and 10 years and a day for the home invasion. So yeah, I guess technically there's blood on my hands. Yeah, I been through this murder shit. They had my name in the headlines and my face all in the fucking paper and shit. That's why I relate to my fucking nigga Double A so much because I understood his pain. I had to let the world see my nigga Double motherfucking A, the convict.

But back to my readers who purchased this book to learn more about Double A. I know you like, "Slim, man, after all the conversations you had with the nigga, what you think about his whole story?" Damn, I should have known that this was coming.

Well in my opinion, I think the homie was a killer. In my world, we feel sympathy for killers. I don't know if the homie was gay or not and that's the honest truth. If he was gay, would I have still been cool with him? Man honestly, yeah being that I'm not homophobic or no shit. If you gay, you gay. I know I'm not gay and don't try that gay shit with me and we good. I know a lot of niggas that's gay on some homo thug shit just being honest. Shit you may be one - laugh out loud!

I know you want to hear why I think he killed himself. Well, it was rumors that when he beat the two bodies he has a conversation with his lawyer. There was some talk about this Massachusetts law. Something about if you in the process of appealing your conviction and you was to die, you are considered innocent or some shit like that. Anyway, I think the courts had Double A's money tied up and the only way he could get it was to flip the life sentence or die.

I don't know... Maybe the talk with his lawyer clarified his money position and maybe he thought about the situation. Would you want your family with your riches? Or would you rather the victim family, government, or whoever else with your shit. Rumor has it, he found out that if something happens to him, his family gets that money. What you think happened?

Hint: "For God so loved the world, he gave his only begotten son." John 3:16

THE END

About the Author

Keiko "O.G. Kayko" Thomas aka "Slim" is currently housed at Souza Baranowski aka "The Max." Slim is serving a 17 to 19-year prison sentence with a 10 year and a day sentence running concurrently. He pleads guilty in 2016 to Manslaughter and Home Invasion. He is the founder and CEO of the company Inmate Link, Inc. and Penitentiary Rich, LLC. He is an artist/entertainer, motivational speaker, and life coach. Living by his motto "It's up 2 you," he has become a household name inside the prison world. Not to mention, he's Penitentiary Rich.

You can contact Slim at:
www.corrlinks.com
Keiko Thomas #W108727
Souza Baranowski Correctional Center
PO Box 8000
Shirley, MA 01464

Instagram: @O.G.Kayko

Made in the USA
Columbia, SC
27 February 2025